A SALISBU

CW00555277

THE PEI

1   BATH
2   SALISBURY
3   WELLS
4   OXFORD

*More titles to follow; for a full list and for a
catalogue of all our titles please contact:*

Ex Libris Press
1 The Shambles
Bradford on Avon
Wiltshire, BA15 1JS
Tel/Fax 01225 863595

*Cover: Poultry Cross;
Overleaf: Salisbury Cathedral*

PEDLAR'S PACK 2

A
SALISBURY
ASSORTMENT

collected and presented
by
JOHN CHANDLER

Illustrations by Simon Gane

EX LIBRIS PRESS

Published in 1996 by
EX LIBRIS PRESS
1 The Shambles
Bradford on Avon
Wiltshire
BA15 1JS

Design and typesetting by
Ex Libris Press

Cover printed by Shires Press, Trowbridge
Printed and bound by Cromwell Press, Melksham

ISBN 0 948578 80 7

Contents ~

Salisbury in a Nutshell ~

This book is an anthology, a collection of some of the most intriguing and most evocative writing about Salisbury, in poetry and prose, from medieval times to the twentieth century. Perhaps you are already very familiar with the history of Salisbury. If so, you will recognize the characters and places which turn up in the following pages. If not, here stripped to essentials, is what you need to remember:

☞ Salisbury, known also as New Salisbury or New Sarum, was established on a site where no town had existed before, during the thirteenth century.

☞ Its predecessor, Old Sarum, was a prehistoric hillfort, around, beside and within which Roman, Saxon and Norman towns were built. During the eleventh and twelfth centuries a castle and cathedral co-existed uneasily within Old Sarum's ramparts. Friction between them was probably responsible for the move to Salisbury.

☞ Salisbury Cathedral, apart from its spire (which is a little later) was built continuously from 1220 until about 1270. It is famous throughout the world for the purity of its architecture, and for its remarkable spire, the tallest in England.

☞ Houses for the cathedral clergy and officials were built around the cathedral in a spacious Close (later walled). The Close, which displays fine and fashionable architecture of many periods, has retained its aloofness from its neighbour, the planned city of Salisbury.

☞ Medieval Salisbury grew rich and populous as a cloth manufacturing centre, and as a thriving market town. It had become by the fifteenth century the regional capital of central southern England.

☞ Despite a period of stagnation Salisbury remained an important city, with assize courts, an infirmary, training college, prestigious shops, and a vigorous social and cultural life.

☞ Salisbury has attracted pilgrims and tourists (including writers) since the middle ages. As well as Old Sarum, the cathedral and its Close, visitors have been attracted by the market place and grid pattern of streets, which until the nineteenth century were drained by open water channels. The tourist industry continues to flourish.

All of this you will find elaborated in the following pages. At the end there is a short miscellany of explanations of some of the more obscure references which may trip you up, details of sources, and a brief index.

John Chandler
East Knoyle, May 1996

The High Street, looking south.

Salisbury begins at Old Sarum, and that is where we must go first. The nineteenth century is drawing to a close, and an aesthetic young tourist, the poet Richard Le Gallienne, has hired a boat in Salisbury, to row himself up the Avon.

I AM UPON THE RIVER, and as I leave bathers and other disturbers of the rural peace behind, and pull more and more into the upper reaches of quietness, a curious green hill begins to loom on my left, one circular mound upon another, flanked by grassy hummocks, and approached by grassy causeways. This is Old Sarum, once a Roman camp, then a Saxon town, a cathedral city till 1258, in 1735 a rotten borough capable of returning the elder Pitt, now a haunted rabbit-warren and the most fascinating buried city out of a fairy tale.

If you moor your boat, and walk the intervening fields, you find that the place is even more preserved in plan and foundations than it seemed at the distance. Great moats, with trees growing deep down in them, run round the base, and are spanned by causeways which lead up at last quite steeply to the circular plateau, perhaps some three acres in extent, where stood the old camp, and later the Cathedral, of which a fragment still remains. This fragment of stone wall makes one, so to speak, a little company, suggesting builders comparatively close at hand in history; but else those grass-muffled contours of the old earthworks affect one with peculiar lonesomeness - a dread of the great deep of the past, such as one has of the great deep of space, the same shudder that goes through one as we look down from a dizzy height.

One clutches at the thought of Pitt and his constituents as at a handrail - or one recalls such a tag of history as that here on this forsaken, but still consecrated, ground, was drawn up that 'Ordinal of Offices for the Use of Sarum', which was our first English Prayer Book. This is really a much more important place in history than that splendid grandchild yonder - which has had no history to speak of - though nothing is afoot here but the growing of the grass and the breeding of minor animals, while yonder they are at evensong before a jewelled shrine. But, as you think of that, that ghostly Cathedral begins to rise about you, and a dead monk is a peculiarly startling form of departed spirit.

As one hurries back to one's little boat, the old moats are already filling with night, and early shadows are trooping along the causeways. Soon it will be very dark, and very still, at Old Sarum.

The awesome presence of the foundered town has provoked a variety of responses. For Samuel Pepys the diarist, in 1668, it was fear.

SO ALL OVER THE PLAIN by the sight of the steeple (the plain high and low) to Salsbury by night but before came to the town I saw a great fortification and there light and to it and in it and find it prodigious so as to fright me to be in it all alone at that time of night it being dark. I understand it since to be that that is called Old Sarum.

For the journalist and traveller (and author of Robinson Crusoe*) Daniel Defoe, some fifty years later, Old Sarum was a symbol of political malaise.*

NEAR IT IS ONE FARM-HOUSE, and that is all which is left of this antient city: yet this is called the Borough of Old Sarum, and sends two members to Parliament, who are chosen by the proprietors of certain lands. Whom those members can justly say they represent, would however be hard for them to answer.

And this theme was taken up by that vitriolic political campaigner William Cobbett, who hurled abuse at the hill when he rode past in 1826.

WHEN I CAME DOWN to Stratford Dean, I wanted to go across to Laverstoke, which lay to my left of Salisbury; but just on the side of the road here, at Stratford Dean, rises the ACCURSED HILL. It is very lofty. It was originally a hill in an irregular sort of sugar-loaf shape: but, it was so altered by the Romans, or by somebody, that the upper three-quarter parts of the hill now, when seen from a distance, somewhat resemble three cheeses, laid one upon another; the bottom one a great deal broader than the next, and the top one like a Stilton cheese, in proportion to a Gloucester one. I resolved to ride over this ACCURSED HILL. As I was going up a field towards it, I met a man going home from work. I asked how he got on. He said, very badly. I asked him what was the cause of it. He said the hard times. 'What times,' said I; 'was there ever a finer summer, a finer harvest, and is there not an old wheat-rick in every farm-yard?' 'Ah!' said he, 'they make it bad for poor people, for all that.' 'They?' said I, 'who is they?' He was silent. 'Oh, no no! my friend,' said I, 'it is not they; it is that ACCURSED HILL that has robbed you of the supper that you ought to find smoking on the table when you get home.' I gave him the price of a pot of beer, and on I went, leaving the poor dejected assemblage of skin and bone to wonder at my words.

The hill is very steep, and I dismounted and led my horse up. Being as near to the top as I could conveniently get, I stood a little while reflecting, not so much on the changes which that hill had seen, as on the changes, the terrible changes, which, in all human probability, it had yet to see, and which it would have greatly helped to produce. It was impossible to stand on this accursed spot, without swelling with indignation against the base and plundering and murderous sons of corruption. I have often wished, and I, speaking out loud, expressed the wish now; 'May that man perish for ever and ever, who, having the power, neglects to bring to justice the perjured, the suborning, the insolent and perfidious miscreants, who openly sell their country's rights and their own souls.'

Old Sarum

Old Sarum lost all its political power as a 'rotten borough' in 1832, just six years after being harangued by Cobbett. Then less aggressive visitors, such as the parson-poet William Bowles on a spring day in 1834, could contemplate its more spiritual significance. Bowles, as a canon of Salisbury Cathedral, had a professional interest.

HERE stood the city of the dead; look round -
Dost thou not mark a visionary band,
Druids and bards upon the summits stand,
Of the majestic and time-hallowed mound?
Hark! heard ye not at times the acclaiming word
Of harps, as when those bards, in white array,
Hailed the ascending lord of light and day!

Here, o'er the clouds, the first cathedral rose,
Whose prelates now in yonder fane repose,
Among the mighty of years passed away;
For there her latest seat Religion chose,
There still to heaven ascends the holy lay,
And never may those shrines in dust and silence close!

For centuries people had puzzled over the circumstances of its desertion, and the move down to New Sarum, or Salisbury. The first great investigator of the English landscape, the Tudor courtier John Leland, investigated the matter when he visited in 1542.

SUM THINK that lak of water caussid the inhabitantes to relinquisch the place; yet were ther many welles of swete water. Sum say, that after that in tyme of civile warres that castelles and waullid townes wer kept that the castellanes of Old-Saresbyri and the chanons could not agre, insomuch that the castellanes apon a tyme prohibited them cumming home from Procession and Rogation to re-entre the town. Wherapon the bisshop and they consulting togither at the last began a chirch on their own propre soyle: and then the people resortid strait to New-Saresbyri and buildid ther: and then in continuaunce were a great numbre of the houses of Old-Saresbyri pullid doun and set up at New-Saresbyri.

Popular versions of the legends must always have been
circulating, and gradually they became more fanciful and
elaborate. By 1713 they made a rollicking good story —
not quite matched by the poet's ability to versify it.

OLD SARUM was built on a dry barren Hill,
    A great many years ago,
'Twas a Roman town of strength and renown,
    As its stately ruins show.

Therein was a castle for men of arms,
    And a cloyster for men of the gown;
There were friars and monks, and liars and punks,
    Tho' not any whose names are come down.

The soldier and church-men did not long agree,
    For the surly men with the hilt on,
Made sport at the gate, with the priests that came late
    From shriving the nuns of Wilton.

Whereupon Bishop Poor went to the King,
    And told him his piteous tale,
That rather than abide such a thorn in his side,
    He'd build a new church in the vale.

I'll build a new church in the vale, said he,
    If your highness will give me scope:
Who, I, said the King? I'll not do such a thing
    Without our old father the Pope.

Then I'll go to that whore, reply'd Bishop Poor,
    With a purse full of old gold;
For why should I beg, and make a low leg,
    Where every thing is to be sold?

He went, he prevail'd; he return'd in a trice,
    With ample authority seiz'd,
To remove Sarum-stones, and St Osmund's bones,
    And to build a new church where he pleas'd.

To the Abbess of Wilton he shewed his bull,
    And how much he was in the Pope's grace;
And they two consulted their bellies full,
    Yet they could not agree of a place.

One time as the prelate lay on his down-bed,
    Recruiting his spirits with rest,
There appear'd, as 'tis said, a beautiful maid,
    With her own dear babe at her breast.

To him thus she spoke (the day was scarce broke,
    And his eyes yet to slumber did yield)
Go build me a church without any delay,
    Go build it in Merry-field.

He awakes and he rings; up ran monks and friars
    At the sound of his little bell;
I must know, said he, where Merry-field is;
    But the Devil-a-bit could they tell.

Full early he arose on a morning grey,
    To meditate, and to walk,
And by chance overheard a soldier on the guard,
    As he thus to his fellow did talk.

I will lay on the side of my good yewen bow,
    That I shoot clean over the corn,
As far as that cow in Merry-field,
    Which grazes under the thorn.

Then the bishop cry'd out, Where is Merry-field?
    For his mind was still on his vow:
The soldier reply'd, by the river-side,
    Where you see that brindle-cow.

Upon this he declared his pious intent,
    And about the indulgences ran,
And brought in bad people to build a good steeple,
    And thus the cathedral began.

The principal stones, in a fortunate hour
    For the Pope, King, and some of the peers,
Were laid by Pandulfo's legantine power,
    And 'twas finish'd in thirty years.

Then the men of Old Sarum came down
    From their hill where there was neither well nor spring,
That they might have a mill, and water at will,
    And hear the sweet fishes sing.

Not perhaps the rhymester's happiest achievement, that last line, but in a curious way Dr Walter Pope was following a very long tradition of hyperbole. While the move was actually taking place, and Salisbury Cathedral being built, a court poet, one Henry of Avranches, penned a verse description, in Latin. Here are extracts, in a prose translation, depicting the site of Salisbury as a veritable paradise.

A SUITABLE place for the city's move was sought with great care and soon found. The chosen valley bears fruit in abundance and life-giving streams, and the nearby wood is well endowed for hunting. The forest teems with wild creatures, as well as trees in large numbers, and the creatures thrive even more than the trees. The tree bursts into leaf, and the animal rejoices.

The trees abound in fruit, but the animals produce no fright. The hind has no fear of the bear, nor the stag of the lion. The snake is no terror to the lynx, nor the wolf to the roe-deer. Where the river meadows nurture the woodland shrubs you may watch the birds compete in song. Sometimes it is the nightingale, more often the lark, which outpours its great aria from that tiny throat. The lark celebrates her surroundings, and the nightingale's sweet refrain is a song of love...

But the splendour of the birds, the thronging wildlife and the ubiquitous woods are all outstripped by the fields of fertile soil. Yellow crocus, white lily, dark blue violet, and crimson rose, all here thrive. The deep rich valley brings forth springs and streams, and fish and birds feed in their clear water. Sweet fruitfulness bears flowers and trees, and the moist earth rears grass and corn. Here the flowers and grass are bedecked with dew. The dew is warm, water drenches the gleaming flowers, and the grass grows green. In all the world it was such a home as this that Nature, child of her teeming mother, sought long ago.

Here a new sanctuary, of matchless beauty on a commanding site, is being raised by the workmen's labour. The former house was both high and low, this one is still higher and lower — higher in its standing but on a lower site. Its lowness of site is equalled by the highness of its status. Next to where the building takes shape a living spring bubbles forth, its water surpassing all other. Lighter than a spark, brighter than crystal, purer than gold, sweeter than ambrosia, is this liquid. And so the new church sits where the rushing river gladdens a city, and feeds its citizens with produce a-plenty. The king's woods furnish the houses, the beauty of the flowers comforts the sick, and the vigour of the grass drives away weeds.

If Adam, when cast out of Paradise, had come here, he would have preferred exile rather than his own country... Fortunate indeed are those who will live to see the church completed, how wonderful the sight after so much labour. May the king grant the materials, the bishop his aid, and the masons their labour. These three are needed if the building is to stand. For when it is built it will reflect the might of the king, the love of the bishop, and the trust of the workmen.

And so Old Sarum was deserted, and its secrets slipped under its hill. Until, that is, a programme of excavations was begun in 1909. For a naturalist, such as W.H. Hudson, this was a form of vandalism.

THAT ANCIENT, beautiful carcass, which had long made their mouths water, on which they have now fallen like a pack of hungry hyenas to tear off the old hide of green turf and burrow down to open to the light or drag out the deep, stony framework. The beautiful surrounding thickets, too, must go, they tell me, since you cannot turn the hill inside out without destroying the trees and bushes that crown it. What person who has known it and has often sought that spot for the sake of its ancient associations, and of the sweet solace they have found in the solitude, or for the noble view of the sacred city from its summit, will not deplore this fatal amiability of the authorities, this weak desire to please everyone and inability to say no to such a proposal!

One writer who visited the excavations and felt moved by the discoveries, was Ella Noyes. Her book on Salisbury Plain was published in 1913.

WANDERING among the bared ruins one day, we chanced upon an excavator crouched upon the ground busily scraping. With his clever fingers and tool he deftly unearthed close beneath the surface the bones of a man, one by one, and fitted them together with practised eye and hand. The skeleton of a man in early middle life, of good height and with splendid teeth, some soldier of the twelfth century, he opined, shot upon the ramparts by a besieger's arrow, or hanged from the wall, perhaps, for some misdeed, and laid here in a hastily-scratched hole just within the rampart. Several other skeletons have been found so placed. What old tragedies of the sudden death of strong men do these things signify. Earth makes all sweet. The green sod has lightly covered them up through all these centuries, and we who used to walk unawares over them upon the hill-top were only vaguely conscious of their presence by some peculiar lightness and peace in the air, as of sorrow and pain long cleared away.

Fifty years later the tragedy and humanity of those who moved to the new Salisbury and built the new cathedral were powerfully evoked by the novelist, William Golding. In this extract the spire's begetter, Jocelin, Dean of Salisbury, has climbed to the top of the nearly-completed structure, and gazes at the scene around and below him.

AT THE NEARER EDGE of the downs, there were knobs and lumps appearing, as if bushes were growing by magic. As he watched, they pushed up, and became men. Behind them were more knobs which became horses, asses in foal with panniers, a whole procession of travellers with burdens. They came straight over the nearer ridge from the one so bluely outlined behind it. They were moving straight down the hill towards his eye, towards the tower, the cathedral, the city. They had not gone by the west, circling down by Cold Harbour to make their way slanting along the deep trench that generations of hooves had cut. They were saving time, if not labour. In a flash of vision he saw how other feet would cut their track arrowstraight towards the city, understood how the tower was laying a hand on the whole landscape, altering it, dominating it, enforcing a pattern that reached wherever the tower could be seen, by sheer force of its being there. He swung round the horizon and saw how true his vision was. There were new tracks, people in parties, making their way sturdily between bushes and through heather. The countryside was shrugging itself obediently into a new shape. Presently, with this great finger sticking up, the city would lie like the hub at the centre of a predestined wheel. New Street, New Inn, New Wharf, New Bridge; and now new roads to bring in new people.

Seldom has the view of the ground from the spire been described, but turning the image round – well, descriptions of the spire from the ground are legion. First, a local poet's impression, Maurice Hewlett, from a volume published in 1920.

WHERE'ER YOU WALK about the shire,
    If you may trust our people,
You'll not escape the arrowy spire
    That beacons Sarum steeple.

Homing the way from Andover
    She smites you thro' the haze;
You round a bluff, and she's so fair
    It fills the heart with praise-

To see her stiff as Aaron's rod,
    Dark in the purple gloom,
Lifting on high a swelling bud
    Not broken into bloom.

She stares against a thundercloud
    As ghastly as a finger
That singles you amidst a crowd
    And will not let you linger;

Or grows up in an open down
    Like a tall poplar tree:
You look to see her bent and thrown
    As the wind flings his gree.

And far away I've seen her ghost
    Across the hazy acres
A legionary of the host
    Whose poets were their makers.

But best of all, from Harnham meads,
    I see the homes of men
Beneath her shadow hide their heads
    Like chicks below a hen.

She spreads her wings and calls them there
    Safely beneath her height;
They cluster, while in upper air
    The great winds scream and fight.

Brave building there by men of old,
    Exulting and tremendous,
In summer heat or winter cold
    To 'monish or befriend us!

Opposite: Matrons' College

From visitors the first view of the distant spire, and its omnipresence, have always provoked a response. Here are three, from Oliver Wendell Holmes in the 1880s, J.J. Hissey in the 1890s, and J.B. Priestley in the 1930s.

IN MY VARIOUS EXCURSIONS from Salisbury I was followed everywhere by the all-pervading presence of the towering spire. Just what it was in that earlier visit, when my eyes were undimmed and my sensibilities unworn, just such I found it now. As one drives away from the town, the roofs of the houses drop out of the landscape, the lesser spires disappear one by one, until the great shaft is left standing alone, — solitary as the broken statue of Ozymandias in the desert, as the mast of some mighty ship above the waves which have rolled over the foundering vessel.

RETURNING to the dog-cart we passed through a deep chalk cutting, and upon reaching the other side of this a most glorious and far-reaching prospect was revealed to us. Miles upon miles of wooded country lay spread out map-like beneath, interspersed with towns, villages, roads, railways, streams, and mansions surrounded by their parks; beyond all this was a vague distance of blue hills, excepting to the north, where the more level landscape faded away into a dreamy dimness. In the very centre of all this spreading loveliness the thin tapering spire of Salisbury's famous cathedral rose gracefully above the ancient city. 'How beautiful!' we both involuntarily exclaimed, and truly if ever a prospect deserved that appellation, this did.

I have seen many a panorama of exceeding loveliness during my numerous drives through the length and breadth of England, but when all were so beautiful, which was the most so I could not tell. That one revelation of scenery, however, settled the matter. Salisbury's soaring spire, with its graceful, arrowlike rise into the air, gives a special character to the view, that makes it, in my opinion, the finest in England.

AND SO the journey turned into a most pleasant and satisfying experience. It reached its peak when we crossed the spur of the Downs, looked into the distant vale and saw, far away in the autumnal haze, the spire of Salisbury Cathedral like a pointed finger, faintly luminous. This is a noble view of England, and Constable himself could not have contrived a better light for it. You have before you a

Shakespearean landscape, with shreds of Arden all about it, glimpses of parks of Navarre, and Illyrian distances. So we descended upon Salisbury.

The view becomes a canvas, in Priestley's imagination, to be compared with Constable's famous painting. W.H. Hudson could paint a picture in a few sentences.

THE ARTIST'S favourite point is from the meadows; there, from the waterside, you have the cathedral not too far away nor too near for a picture, whether on canvas or in the mind, standing amidst its great old trees, with nothing but the moist green meadows and the river between. One evening, during the late summer of this wettest season, when the rain was beginning to cease, I went out this way for my stroll, the pleasantest if not the only 'walk' there is in Salisbury. The rain ceased, but the sky was still stormy, with a great blackness beyond the cathedral and still other black clouds coming up from the west behind me. Then the sun, near its setting, broke out, sending a flame of orange colour through the dark masses around it, and at the same time flinging a magnificent rainbow on that black cloud against which the immense spire stood wet with rain and flushed with light, so that it looked like a spire built of a stone impregnated with silver. Never had Nature so glorified man's work! It was indeed a marvellous thing to see, an effect so rare that in all the years I had known Salisbury, and the many times I had taken that stroll in all weathers, it was my first experience of such a thing. How lucky, then, was Constable to have seen it, when he set himself to paint his famous picture! And how brave he was and even wise to have attempted such a subject, one which, I am informed by artists with the brush, only a madman would undertake, however great a genius he might be.

But such perfection in art can pall, as Henry James shrewdly observed.

IT IS PERHAPS the best-known typical church in the world, thanks to its shapely spire; but the spire is so simply and obviously fair that when you have respectfully made a note of it you have anticipated aesthetic analysis. I had seen it before and admired it heartily, and perhaps I should have done as well to let my admiration rest. I confess that on repeated inspection it grew to seem to me the least bit banal, or even bête, since I am talking French, and I began to consider whether it does not belong to the same range of art as the Apollo Belvedere or the Venus de' Medici. I am inclined to think that if I had to live within sight of a cathedral and encounter it in my daily comings and goings I should grow less weary of the rugged black front of Exeter than of the sweet perfection of Salisbury. There are people by temperament easily sated with beauties specifically fair, and the effect of Salisbury Cathedral architecturally is equivalent to that of flaxen hair and blue eyes physiognomically.

Hudson, in fact, was inclined to agree.

OCCASIONALLY I met and talked with an old man employed at the cathedral. One day, closing one eye and shading the other with his hand, he gazed up at the building for some time, and then remarked: 'I'll tell you what's wrong with Salisbury — it looks too noo.' He was near the mark; the fault is that to the professional eye it is faultless; the lack of expression is due to the fact that it came complete from its maker's brain, like a coin from the mint, and being all in one symmetrical plan it has the trim, neat appearance of a toy cathedral carved out of wood and set on a green-painted square.

The truth, I suppose, is that what we take from visiting Salisbury Cathedral, as from viewing any work of art, is conditioned by what we bring to it. We may, for example, see it as the embodiment of our religious beliefs. This was Charles Kingsley's experience (with just a hint of worldly pleasures at the end).

I HAVE BEEN WALKING round the cathedral — oh! such a cathedral! Perfect unity, in extreme multiplicity. The first thing which strikes you in it (spiritually, I mean) is its severe and studied calm, even to 'primness' — nothing luscious, very little or no variation. Then you begin to feel how one it is; how the high slated roof and the double lancet windows, and the ranges of graduating lancet arches filling every gable, and the continued repetition of the same simple forms even in the buttresses and string courses, and corbel tables, and the extreme harsh angular simplicity of the mouldings — all are developments of one idea, and the idea so well expressing the tone of its date, the end of the thirteenth and beginning of the fourteenth centuries, I suppose, when the 'revival' of the age of St Francis, St Dominic, and dear St Elizabeth had formed itself, from the many private fancies of its great minds, into one clear dark system of stern, elegant, soul-crushing asceticism. And then from the centre of all this, that glorious spire rises — the work of a slightly later hand — too huge, I believe, for the rest of the cathedral, its weight having split and crushed its supporters. Fit emblem of the result of curbing systems. The moment the tower escapes above the level of the roof, it bursts into the wildest luxuriance, retaining the general character of the building below, but disguising it in a thousand fantastic excrescences — like the mind of man, crushed by human systems, and then suddenly asserting its own will in some burst of extravagance, yet unconsciously retaining the harsh and severe lineaments of the school in which it had been bred. And then its self-willed fancies exhaust themselves, and it makes one final struggle upward, in a vast simple pyramid like that spire; emblem of the return, the revulsion rather, to 'pure' and naked spirituality. And when even that has dwindled to a point, it must end — if it would have either safety, or permanence, or shelter, or beauty — as that spire ends, in the Cross!

Oh! that cathedral is an emblem, unconscious to its builders, of the whole history of Popery from the twelfth century to the days when Luther preached once more Christ crucified for us! — For ever above us, yet for ever among us.

That cathedral has one peculiar beauty. It rises sheer out of a smooth and large grass field, not struggling up among chimneys and party-walls, but with the grass growing to the foot of the plinth. Those blundering Iconoclasts have knocked the beautiful west front to pieces. I hope they meant well: I fear not.

It is lucky I took down my tackle, for I am promised a day's trout fishing to-morrow. Oh! lucky me!...

High Street Gate, from the Close

*For another Victorian writer, Thomas Hardy, the west front
seemed to confirm his own rationalist views.*

Along the sculptures of the western wall
    I watched the moonlight creeping:
It moved as if it hardly moved at all,
    Inch by inch thinly peeping
Round on the pious figures of freestone, brought
And poised there when the Universe was wrought
To serve its centre, Earth, in mankind's thought.

The lunar look skimmed scantly toe, breast, arm,
    Then edged on slowly, slightly,
To shoulder, hand, face; till each austere form
    Was blanched its whole length brightly
Of prophet, king, queen, cardinal in state,
That dead men's tools had striven to simulate;
And the stiff images stood irradiate.

A frail moan from the martyred saints there set
    Mid others of the erection
Against the breeze, seemed sighings of regret
    At the ancient faith's rejection
Under the sure, unhasting, steady stress
Of Reason's movement, making meaningless
The coded creeds of old-time godliness.

William Cobbett, still angry after his visit to Old Sarum, approached the cathedral with his usual robust indignation.

YESTERDAY MORNING I went into the Cathedral at Salisbury about 7 o'clock. When I got into the nave of the church, and was looking up and admiring the columns and the roof, I heard a sort of humming, in some place which appeared to be in the transept of the building. I wondered what it was, and made my way towards the place whence the noise appeared to issue. As I approached it, the noise seemed to grow louder. At last, I thought I could distinguish the sounds of the human voice. This encouraged me to proceed; and, still following the sound, I at last turned in at a doorway to my left, where I found a priest and his congregation assembled. It was a parson of some sort, with a white covering on him, and five women and four men: when I arrived, there were five couple of us. I joined the congregation, until they came to the litany; and then, being monstrously hungry, I did not think myself bound to stay any longer. I wonder what the founders would say, if they could rise from the grave, and see such a congregation as this in this most magnificent and beautiful cathedral. I wonder what they would say, if they could know to what purpose the endowments of this Cathedral are now applied; and above all things, I wonder what they would say, if they could see the half-starved labourers that now minister to the luxuries of those who wallow in the wealth of those endowments... For my part,

I could not look up at the spire and the whole of the church at Salisbury, without feeling that I lived in degenerate times. Such a thing never could be made now. We feel that, as we look at the building. It really does appear that if our forefathers had not made these buildings, we should have forgotten, before now, what the Christian religion was!

ॐ

For Daniel Defoe, the cathedral's fascination lay in how it was built, and some curious statistics.

THEY TELL US here long stories of the great art used in laying the first foundation of this church, the ground being marshy and wet, occasioned by the chanels of the rivers; that it was laid upon piles, according to some; and upon woolpacks, according to others. But this is not to be believed by those who know, that the whole country is one rock of chalk, even from the tops of the highest hills, to the bottom of the deepest rivers. And the foundation of woolpacks is, no doubt, allegorical, and has respect to the woollen trade.

The ordinary boast of this building, in the following verses, must not be omitted:

As many Days as in One Year there be,
So many Windows in One Church we see;
As many Marble Pillars there appear,
As there are Hours throughout the fleeting Year;
As many Gates as Moons One Year do view:
Strange Tale to tell, yet not more strange than true!

This was a well-known calculation, even in the seventeenth century. Thomas Fuller quoted it, and recalled this encounter.

ONCE WALKING in this church (whereof then I was prebendary) I met a countryman wondering at the structure thereof. 'I once', said he to me, 'admired that there could be a church that should have so many pillars as there be hours in the year; and now I admire more that there should be so many hours in the year as I see pillars in this church.'

But even this marvel could be capped. Miss Child, one of that tribe of indomitable Close ladies whom we shall encounter shortly, had done some further calculations.

THERE'S ANOTHER coincidence, curious and strange,
Which most surely no mind could invent or arrange;
The sole cause must have been unaccountable chance
While the builders proceeded their work to advance;
For, to say the strict truth, I'm by no means aware
That the true statute mile was then measured with care.
And perhaps, the detail may be read with a smile,
That this Church, in exterior, metes just half a mile.
 Such tradition was extant — by many believed,
And great pains I have taken that none be deceived:
I've employed shrewd mechanics its angles to trace,
That no doubt may exist on this singular case.
These my bidding obeyed, both with line and with rule,

And full many an useful and well-managed tool:
Thus they measured round buttresses, flying and straight,
By the large eastern window — across the west gate;
Round its corners, and niches, and pillars they pace,
With the transepts which give it such beauty and grace.
The result of this labour has proved beyond doubt
That it measures one-half of a mile round about;
Or eight hundred and eighty yards, being the same,
To give one title more to its widely-spread fame.

Even without such statistics, the sheer size of the cathedral compared with the houses around it, was a frequent cause of wonderment. As Edith Olivier, another Close lady, recalled:

THE CONTRAST between what they thought fitting as a House of God and as a house of man recalls a remark made by a little boy of three who, looking up at the cathedral for the first time, said, 'They must have had a lot of stuff to build that big church'. They had indeed.

Charles Kingsley compared the cathedral to a mountain.

I HAVE BEEN WANDERING in and out of that wonderful grey Alp among the trees. I could write a volume on it. it is like Raffaelle's Belle Jardiniere — perfect lofty grace, without a touch of severity. It is like a great mountain, with its strata, and secondary ridges, and spurs, and lower peaks, all leading up to that great central aiguille which rushes up into the highest blue, till you expect to see the clouds hanging round its top, and fancy the jackdaws are condors round the peak of Chimborazo.

American visitors, which Salisbury is never lacking, have been among the most perceptive and entertaining of commentators. For some years the official guide to Salisbury carried on its title-page the slogan, 'the apple of the eye of England'. This was not some advertising agency's invention. The source was the nineteenth-century American poet, essayist and medical professor, Oliver Wendell Holmes. He revisited England as an old man in 1886, and published his observations the following year.

SALISBURY CATHEDRAL was my first love among all the wonderful ecclesiastical buildings which I saw during my earlier journey. I looked forward to seeing it again with great anticipations of pleasure, which were more than realized.

If one had to name the apple of the eye of England, I

think he would be likely to say that Salisbury Cathedral was as near as he could come to it, and that the white of the eye was Salisbury Close. The cathedral is surrounded by a high wall, the gates of which, — its eyelids, — are closed every night at a seasonable hour, at which the virtuous inhabitants are expected to be in their safe and sacred quarters. Houses within this hallowed precinct naturally bring a higher rent than those of the unsanctified and unprotected region outside of its walls. It is a realm of peace, glorified by the divine edifice, which lifts the least imaginative soul upward to the heavens its spire seems trying to reach; beautified by rows of noble elms which stretch high aloft, as if in emulation of the spire; beatified by holy memories of the good and great men who have worn their lives out in the service of the church of which it is one of the noblest temples.

Yes, American visitors seem always to have been fascinated by the peculiar Englishness of the Close. Nathaniel Hawthorne, in 1863, began to daydream about it.

I NEVER BEHELD anything — I must say again — so cosey, so indicative of domestic comfort for whole centuries together, — houses so fit to live in or to die in, and where it would be so pleasant to lead a young wife beneath the antique portal, and dwell with her till husband and wife were patriarchal, — as these delectable old houses. They belong naturally to the cathedral, and have a necessary relation to it, and its sanctity is somehow thrown over them all, so that they do not quite belong to this world, though they look full to overflowing of whatever earthly things are good for man. These are places, however, in which mankind makes no progress; the rushing tumult of human life here subsides into a deep, quiet pool, with perhaps a gentle circular eddy, but no onward movement. The same identical thought, I suppose, goes round in a slow whirl from one generation to another, as I have seen a withered leaf do in the vortex of a brook.

The truth of his remarks is borne out by one such resident, Edith Olivier, writing nearly eighty years later.

THE PEOPLE in the Close were then (and doubtless still are) greatly influenced by their houses. No one living in these can ever be quite commonplace. Very few of our

The Chapter House

neighbours went to bed without first looking through their windows out into the moonlight or the starlight, to find against the sky the outline of the cathedral, standing apart upon its great sweep of lawn — a silent beatitude. Month by month they watched the stars in their courses journeying in their gigantic wheels over the spire. On summer evenings, the groups which stood gossiping in the Close over the little events of the day, were never altogether oblivious of the beauty of the glowing twilight as it slowly blurred the noble lines and the intricate carvings of the great building.

The people who lived in the Close presented a unique combination of elsewhere incompatible attitudes towards their houses. In the first place, they took them entirely as a matter of course. There seemed to them nothing remarkable in the fact that they had been chosen by Divine Decree to run in and out to their tea-parties through those supremely beautiful doorways. That — so it seemed to those scholarly canons and gentle old maids — is what the houses are like in which one lives. Then there was the other point of view. Their natural acquiescence in their good fortune never blinded them to the beauty of their surroundings. No-one in the Close was surprised if a passing visitor asked permission to look inside the door and into the rooms. Such visits seemed as natural as the milkman's daily call. The lot had fallen unto them in a fair ground and they knew it; but they were house-conscious rather than house-proud. This peculiar spirit of the Close is difficult to describe, but it is one of the first things which strikes one on coming to live there.

And what could be more in the spirit of the Close than a Victorian parson nodding off, on a seat in front of the cathedral? Charles Kingsley in 1857.

BUT THE REPOSE is so wonderful. You shut your eyes, and re-open them with a sort of surprise at finding it still there. It awes you, too, without crushing you. You can be cheerful under its shadow, but you could not do a base thing. But I will not ramble on...

Why ever not? That's what we expect of a Victorian parson. And life in the Close rambled on, as one great historian of Victorian England, G.M. Young, has pointed out.

YET IN THE FAR DISTANCE I can well conceive the world turning wistfully in imagination, as to the culminating achievement of European culture, to the life of the University-bred classes in England of the mid-nineteenth century, set against the English landscape as it was, as it can be no more, but of which, nevertheless, some memorials remain with us today, in the garden at Kelmscott, in the hidden valleys of the Cotswolds, in that walled close where all the pride and piety, the peace and beauty of a vanished world seem to have made their last home under the spire of St Mary of Salisbury.

*The quintessential spokesman of educated mid-Victorian
family life was perhaps the poet Coventry Patmore. He
fondly remembered spending Christmas at the Deanery.*

ONCE MORE I came to Sarum Close,
    With joy half memory, half desire,
And breathed the sunny wind that rose
    And blew the shadows o'er the Spire,
And toss'd the lilac's scented plumes,
    And sway'd the chestnut's thousand cones,
And fill'd my nostrils with perfumes,
    And shaped the clouds in waifs and zones,
And wafted down the serious strain
    Of Sarum bells, when, true to time,
I reach'd the Dean's, with heart and brain
    That trembled to the trembling chime.

'Twas half my home, six years ago.
    The six years had not alter'd it:
Red-brick and ashlar, long and low,
    With dormers and with oriels lit.
Geranium, lychnis, rose array'd
    The windows, all wide open thrown;
And some one in the Study play'd
    The Wedding-March of Mendelssohn.
And there it was I last took leave:
    'Twas Christmas: I remember'd now
The cruel girls, who feign'd to grieve,
    Took down the evergreens; and how

The holly into blazes woke
    The fire, lighting the large, low room,
A dim, rich lustre of old oak
    And crimson velvet's glowing gloom.

St. Ann's Gate

To later generations the Close seemed populated with old-fashioned eccentrics. Here Dorothy Devenish recalls childhood visits early this century from her home in the nearby Woodford valley.

44

ABOUT THE CATHEDRAL precincts fluttered the old minor canons, too absorbed in intimate, ritualistic life to notice the tourists or other evidence of the twentieth century. Sometimes, seated in their crowded drawing-rooms, I have looked out through the windows and watched the cathedral towering above me. The dizzy, multifariously carved pile of stone would seem poised ready to fall in avenging wrath upon the dwellers in the little house if they dared challenge the doctrines which it so proudly affirmed. It dwarfed the trees and shut out the sky, yet seemed to derive from the shadows and sunlight a strange, vibrant life of its own. At those moments I understood how it could become for some a master as exacting as could a few acres of land for others. I also understood why some of the young things brought up in its shadow accentuated their own personalities with Hollywood manners, blood-red nails, and confused love affairs! In earlier generations also the strain had sometimes proved too great, and there were usually to be found, wandering about the precincts, little gentle old ladies who let their scraggy grey locks, crowned with artificial roses, fall in would-be ringlets down their backs, or otherwise defied convention, a late and inadequate gesture against their frustration. Such people were regarded without surprise or consternation, and went their harmless way leaving behind them a splash of colour and a vague surmise.

Some of the Close characters lived in St Nicholas's Hospital, a charitable institution by the river just beyond Harnham Gate. It was discovered by Anthony Trollope when he explored Salisbury in 1851, and it provided him with the inspiration for the community around which the first of his Barchester novels revolves.

HIRAM'S Hospital, as the retreat is called, is a picturesque building enough, and shows the correct taste with which the ecclesiastical architects of those days were imbued. It stands on the banks of the little river, which flows nearly round the cathedral close, being on the side furthest from the town. The London road crosses the river by a pretty one-arched bridge, and, looking from this bridge, the stranger will see the windows of the old men's rooms, each pair of windows separated by a small buttress. A broad gravel walk runs between the building and the river, which is always trim and cared for; and at the end of the walk, under the parapet of the approach to the bridge, is a large and well-worn seat, on which, in mild weather, three or four of Hiram's bedesmen are sure to be seen seated. Beyond this row of buttresses, and further from the bridge, and also further from the water which here suddenly bends, are the pretty oriel windows of Mr Harding's house, and his well-mown lawn. The entrance to the hospital is from the London road, and is made through a ponderous gateway under a heavy stone arch, unnecessary, one would suppose, at any time, for the protection of twelve old men, but greatly conducive to the good appearance of Hiram's charity. On passing through this portal, never closed to anyone from 6 a.m. till 10 p.m., and never open afterwards, except on application to a huge, intricately hung medieval bell, the handle of which no unitiated intruder can possibly find, the six doors of the old men's abodes are seen, and beyond them is a slight iron screen, through which the more happy portion of the Barchester elite pass into the Elysium of Mr Harding's dwelling.

How far Hiram's was modelled on St Nicholas's Hospital, by Harnham Bridge in Salisbury, is a matter of debate. But a few hundred yards away, in front of the cathedral, stands another medieval building immortalized in a Victorian novel. Now Salisbury Museum, in Thomas Hardy's day it was a college for women teachers. There he sent one of his tragic heroines, Sue Bridehead.

THE SEVENTY young women, of ages varying in the main from nineteen to one-and-twenty, though several were older, who at this date filled the species of nunnery known as the Training-School at Melchester, formed a very mixed community, which included the daughters of mechanics, curates, surgeons, shopkeepers, farmers, dairymen, soldiers, sailors, and villagers. They sat in the large school-room of the establishment on the evening previously described, and word was passed round that Sue Bridehead had not come in at closing-time.

'She went out with her young man,' said a second-year's

student, who knew about young men. 'And Miss Traceley saw her at the station with him. She'll have it hot when she does come.'

She said he was her cousin,' observed a youthful new girl.

That excuse has been made a little too often in this school to be effectual in saving our souls,' said the head girl of the year, drily.

The fact was that, only twelve months before, there had occurred a lamentable seduction of one of the pupils, who had made the same statement in order to gain meetings with her lover. The affair had created a scandal, and the management had consequently been rough on cousins ever since.

*Sue was one of three Hardy characters who came to
emotional grief in Salisbury. The city, in fact, seems to
have been pretty rough on affairs of the heart generally.
Or so Richard Le Gallienne, whom we left rowing
downstream from Old Sarum, would have us believe.*

MR LANG tells how once a train in which he travelled
stopping at Salisbury, a sad middle-aged lady in the
carriage turned to another sad middle-aged lady and said:
'Poor Jane! she had reason to remember Salisbury'. And
Mr Lang goes on to say how that remark continued to
tease his mind, and how often afterwards he had wondered
why it was that 'Jane' should so particularly remember
Salisbury. I write 'Jane'. The lady's name may have been
another. That is no matter. I thought of her as Jane as I
entered the old city an hour or so from dinner-time; for, I
too, poor anonymous Jane, have reasons to remember
Salisbury, reasons glad and sad, perhaps all sad now,
because they were once all glad, — reasons for so much
as referring to which I must apologise to the reader.

No, please don't apologise. And, as if to bear out the impression that it could happen to anyone, here is a moving entry from the diary of a Victorian curate from north Wiltshire, the Reverend Francis Kilvert.

IN THE AFTERNOON I preached from the Gospel for the day, [John] xvi.7. 'Nevertheless I tell you the truth. It is expedient for you that I go away.'

I walked on to Kington to help Edward Awdry and preached the same sermon, telling the people at Langley and Kington the sweet sad story of how those words came to me as a token in Salisbury Cathedral on that dark sorrowful winter's day, the 7th of last December, the day I parted from and saw the last of my darling Ettie. I told them how one dark cold snowy day in midwinter a man who had just parted perhaps for ever from his dearest friend came almost broken-hearted to a Cathedral city, and how being delayed there on his journey for some hours he wandered about the cold desolate snowy streets, sick at heart, broken-spirited, well nigh broken-hearted, with the tender loving despairing words of the last farewell ringing

in his ears as he still seemed to feel the last long lingering
pressure of the hand and the last long clinging embrace
and passionate kiss and the latest sorrowful imploring look
and beseeching word, 'Don't forget.' I told them how the
broken-hearted man wandered at length into the Cathedral
close as the short winter twilight was fast passing into
night, and saw the leafless boughs of the elms bare against
the sky and the great spire towering dark amongst the
murky snow clouds and the snow on the Cathedral roof
and the lighted windows of the great Church shining
through the dark and heard the roll of the distant organ
which reminded him that it was the hour of Evensong. I
told them how the sorrowful traveller went into the
Cathedral and how, as he entered, the second lesson for
the day was being read from the 16th Chapter of St John's
Gospel and how the first words that fell on his ear were
those from the 7th verse, 'Nevertheless I tell you the truth.
It is expedient for you that I go away, for if I go not away
the Comforter will not come unto you, but if I depart I
will send Him unto you.'

I told them how the broken-hearted man took the words
as a sign and token from heaven and how they comforted
him greatly for he thought it might be better for his friend
that they had parted and that he had gone away and he
hoped that now his dear friend might be comforted. All
this I told them. But I did not say that I was the broken-
hearted traveller, that the story was my own, and that I
was speaking of one of the great sorrows of my life.

Another visitor in pensive mood was Ernest Walls, who in 1929 published an account of a journey down the Salisbury Avon.

AND AS I STOOD like Trollope on the little bridge above the silver river my own thoughts turned to the pageant of the past, seven hundred years of life in Sarum, a story that stands out in clear-cut cameos, a true epitome of England in each succeeding century. The ambitious churchmen with their great achievements of building and organisation, their dreams of a visible bridge 'twixt earth and heaven; the pious pilgrims; the clashing dynasties; wealthy merchants and jealous citizens; White Rose and Red Rose; Roundhead and Cavalier; Whig and Tory; the elegance of the eighteenth-century Close; each phase in turn has left its lasting mark on Salisbury.

Yet it is neither in the quiet Close nor in the medieval halls nor yet in the great cathedral of Salisbury that its true heart is found. For all those seven hundred years Salisbury has been the city of the Plain, the market and gathering-place of the dwellers in all the villages and hamlets strung along the river valleys that radiate from it. Mute and inarticulate till roused by some fierce injustice, the Wiltshire peasant during all these centuries and as many again has lived on the Wiltshire soil through many changing tenures, himself unchanging. To him to-day, as to his fathers before him, Salisbury is the centre of the world. And as you see him in the busy streets of Salisbury on market day, you realise that Salisbury belongs to him, exists for him and always has done.

After Old Sarum, the cathedral and its Close, visitors to Salisbury generally ventured out to wander through the city. What first caught their eye, until the sanitary Victorians removed them, were the open watercourses which ran along most of the streets. Opinions about their value as an amenity were very mixed.

IN THE CITY of Salisbury doe reigne the dropsy, consumption, scurvy, gowte; it is an exceeding dampish place.

SALISBURY is a large, well-built, and pleasant city; and the founders of it seemed to have run from one extreme to another; for as the old city wanted water, this has rather too much, the water running thro' the middle of every street, which, I think, does not add to the beauty of the town, but just the contrary; for it keeps the streets always dirty, full of wet and filth, and weeds, even in the middle of summer.

I WENT TO SARUM 8 miles which is a Citty a Bishops Seate, pretty large town streetes broad but through the midst of them runs a little rivulet of water which makes the streetes not so clean or so easy to passe in, they have stepp's to cross it and many open places for horses and carriages to cross itt - it takes off much from the beauty of the streets.

THROUGH ONE OR MORE of the streets there runs a

swift, clear little stream, which, being close to the pavement, and bordered with stone, may be called, I suppose, a kennel, though possessing the transparent purity of a rustic rivulet. It is a brook in city garb.

NOR MUST THE INDUSTRY of the citizens of Salisbury be forgotten, who have derived the river in every street therein; so that Salisbury is a heap of islets thrown together. This mindeth me of an epitaph made on Mr Francis Hyde, a native of this city, who died secretary unto the English lieger in Venice:

> Born in the English Venice, thou didst die,
> Dear friend, in the Italian Salisbury.

Mompesson House, The Close

To anyone familiar with nineteenth-century engravings of Salisbury, which depict the watercourses confined within narrow brick culverts, that epithet (quoted by Thomas Fuller in 1662, and often repeated) must seem a gross exaggeration. But until 1737 they were much wider and, if not of Venetian proportions, were nevertheless a considerable obstacle. The recently published journal of a Dutch traveller in 1662, William Schellink, explains.

IN EVERY STREET is a channel of running water 7 or 8 feet wide, of clear, sweet water. In these channels 3 or 4 stones or wooden blocks are set at many places to step on, to cross over the water; the horses go through in the middle and the wheels at the sides of these stepping stones in the water.

For some visitors, their lasting impression of Salisbury was the accommodation afforded them in the city's inns. Samuel Pepys, for instance, was not satisfied.

SO BACK HOME and there being light we to the church and there find them at prayers again so could not see the quire but I sent the women home and I did go in and see very many fine tombs and among the rest some very ancient of the Mountagus. So home to dinner and that being done paid the reckoning which was so exorbitant and perticularly in rate of my horses and 7s 6d for bread and beer that I was mad about it and resolve to trouble the mistress about it and get something for the poor. And came away in that humour.

Others seem to have fared rather better. Here is the Hon John Byng, in 1782.

MOST REFRESHING was the ride to Sarum, the air was so cool, and so sweet; and by the way I saw several deer upon the edge of the chace. - I was at Sarum in time for the hot rolls, and was receiv'd at the White Hart, civilly and attentively; there shaved, and dressed; drank coffee; and then went to survey the cathedral which I had seen before and of which I resumed my old remarks.

Charles Dickens developed the fulsome description of inns into an artform. Here is his treatment of a Salisbury establishment on a snowy night.

AND, LO! the towers of the Old Cathedral rise before them, even now! and by-and-bye they come into the sheltered streets, made strangely silent by their white carpet; and so to the Inn for which they are bound; where they present such flushed and burning faces to the cold waiter, and are so brimful of vigour, that he almost feels assaulted by their presence; and, having nothing to oppose to the attack (being fresh, or rather stale, from the blazing fire in the coffee-room), is quite put out of his pale countenance.

A famous Inn! the hall a very grove of dead game, and dangling joints of mutton; and in one corner an illustrious larder, with glass doors, developing cold fowls and noble joints, and tarts wherein the raspberry jam coyly withdrew itself, as such a precious creature should, behind a lattice work of pastry. And behold, on the first floor, at the court-end of the house, in a room with all the window-curtains drawn, a fire piled half-way up the chimney, plates warming before it, wax candles gleaming everywhere, and a table spread for three, with silver and glass enough for thirty.

And what might be waiting for the newly-arrived traveller beyond the portals of his inn? Dickens again.

MR PINCH had a shrewd notion that Salisbury was a very desperate sort of place; an exceeding wild and dissipated city; and when he had put up the horse, and given the hostler to understand that he would look again in the course of an hour or two to see him take his corn, he set forth on a stroll about the streets with a vague and not unpleasant idea that they teemed with all kinds of mystery and bedevilment. To one of his quiet habits this little delusion was greatly assisted by the circumstance of its being market-day, and the thoroughfares about the market-place being filled with carts, horses, donkeys, baskets, waggons, garden-stuff, meat, tripe, pies, poultry and huckster's wares of every opposite description and possible variety of character Then there were young farmers and old farmers with smock-frocks, brown great-coats, drab great-coats, red worsted comforters, leather-leggings, wonderful shaped hats, hunting-whips, and rough sticks, standing about in groups, or talking noisily together on the tavern steps, or paying and receiving huge amounts of greasy wealth, with the assistance of such bulky pocket-books that when they were in their pockets it was apoplexy to get them out, and when they were out it was spasms to get them in again. Also there were farmers' wives in beaver bonnets and red cloaks, riding shaggy horses purged of all earthly passions, who went soberly into all manner of places without desiring to know why, and who, if required, would have stood stock-still in a china-shop, with a complete dinner-service at each hoof. Also a great many dogs, who were strongly interested in the state of the market and the bargains of their masters and a great confusion of tongues, both brute and human.

Mr Pinch regarded everything exposed for sale with great delight and was particularly struck by the itinerant cutlery, which he considered of the very keenest kind insomuch that he purchased a pocket knife with seven blades in it, and not a cut (as he afterwards found out) among them. When he had exhausted the market-place, and watched the farmers safe into the market dinner, he went back to look after the horse. Having seen him eat unto his heart's content he issued forth again, to wander round the town and regale himself with the shop windows: previously to taking a long stare at the bank, and wondering in what direction underground the caverns might be where they kept the money; and turning to look back at one or two young men who passed him, whom he knew to be articled to solicitors in the town; and who had a sort of fearful interest in his eyes, as jolly dogs who knew a thing or two, and kept it up tremendously.

Fictional characters, such as Tom Pinch, seem always to have happened on Salisbury when it was market-day. One of Hardy's heroes, a young lawyer, was even luckier. His visit coincided with the Michaelmas fair, held then (as now) in the market place.

HE HAD BEEN STANDING in the Close, vainly endeavouring to gain amid the darkness a glimpse of the most homogeneous pile of medieval architecture in England, which towered and tapered from the damp and level sward in front of him. While he stood the presence of the Cathedral walls was revealed rather by the ear than by the eyes; he could not see them, but they reflected sharply a roar of sound which entered the Close by a street leading from the city square, and, falling upon the building, was flung back upon him.

He postponed till the morrow his attempt to examine the deserted edifice, and turned his attention to the noise. It was compounded of steam barrel-organs, the clanging of gongs, the ringing of hand-bells, the clack of rattles, and the undistinguishable shouts of men. A lurid light hung in the air in the direction of the tumult. Thitherward he went, passing under the arched gateway, along a straight street, and into the square.

He might have searched Europe over for a greater contrast between juxtaposed scenes. The spectacle was that of the eighth chasm of the Inferno as to colour and flame, and, as to mirth, a development of the Homeric heaven. A smoky glare, of the complexion of brass-filings, ascended from the fiery tongues of innumerable naphtha lamps affixed to booths, stalls, and other temporary erections which crowded the spacious market-square. In front of this irradiation scores of human figures, more or less in profile, were darting athwart and across, up, down, and around, like gnats against a sunset.

Their motions were so rhythmical that they seemed to be moved by machinery. And it presently appeared that they were moved by machinery indeed; the figures being those of the patrons of swings, see-saws, flying-leaps, above all of the three steam roundabouts which occupied the centre of the position. It was from the latter that the din of steam-organs came.

Throbbing humanity in full light was, on second thoughts, better than architecture in the dark. The young man, lighting a short pipe, and putting his hat on one side and one hand in his pocket, to throw himself into harmony with his new environment, drew near to the largest and most patronized of the steam circuses, as the roundabouts were called by their owners. This was one of brilliant finish, and it was now in full revolution. The musical instrument around which and to whose tones the riders revolved, directed its trumpet-mouths of brass upon the young man, and the long plate-glass mirrors set at angles, which revolved with the machine, flashed the gyrating personages and hobby-horses kaleidoscopically into his eyes.

A large market town such as Salisbury, as Ernest Walls observed earlier, forms a vital and inseparable bond with the villagers of the surrounding countryside. They come in for special occasions, such as the fair, and regularly for shopping. Here is Dorothy Devenish again, recalling her youth.

THE MOST EXCITING day for shopping, though one that was debarred to me, until I attained my own car, by my father's dislike of humanity in the mass and the chauffeur's desire to manoeuvre his large vehicle with a maximum of speed and a minimum of effort — was market day. Then the farmers and workmen and their wives milled about the streets regardless of the ways of modern traffic. The decorum of the banks was unsettled by the clatter of hobnail boots and the voices of men used to conversing

The Poultry Cross

across half an acre. Gruntings, mooings, and lowings floated in through the open door and mixed oddly with the rattle of change and whisper of notes. The inns devoted themselves to 'farmers' ordinaries', where a Pickwickian jollity prevailed and woe betide the unhappy tourist who wanted to be fed! The shopkeepers had to doff their special manner — and price — reserved for 'm'lady' (who only ventured to town on quieter days) and hustle and bustle continuously from morning till night. The estate agents and auctioneers, vital links between the ways of town and country, were busy, important, and happy. Not till the next morning, when the straw and dung were hosed from the market-place, did the town once more belong to the townspeople.

ॐ

And there are other links between city and country, as the perceptive W.H. Hudson described.

THE SELLING and buying; friends and relations to meet in the market-place, and — how often! — the sick one to be seen at the Infirmary. This home of the injured and ailing, which is in the mind of so many of the people gathered together, is indeed the cord that draws and binds the city and the village closest together and makes the two like one.

That great, comely building of warm, red brick in Fisherton Street, set well back so that you can see it as a whole, behind its cedar and beech trees — how familiar it is to the villagers! In numberless humble homes, in hundreds of villages of the Plain, and all over the surrounding country, the 'Infirmary' is a name of the deepest meaning, and a place of many sad and tender and beautiful associations. I heard it spoken of in a manner which surprised me at first, for I know some of the London poor and am accustomed to their attitude towards the metropolitan hospitals.

This country town hospital and infirmary is differently regarded by the villagers of the Plain. It is curious to find how many among them are personally acquainted with it; perhaps it is not easy for anyone, even in this most healthy district, to get through life without sickness, and all are liable to accidents. The injured or afflicted youth, taken straight from his rough, hard life and poor cottage, wonders at the place he finds himself in — the wide, clean, airy room and white, easy bed, the care and skill of the doctors, the tender nursing by women, and comfort and luxuries, all without payment, but given as it seems to him out of pure divine love and compassion — all this comes to him as something strange, almost incredible. He suffers much perhaps, but can bear pain stoically and forget it when it is past, but the loving kindness he has experienced is remembered.

*Closed now, and partly demolished, the old infirmary in
Fisherton Street. But another important institution linking
urban and rural still flourishes. Edith Olivier remembered
the day when she helped to open it.*

THERE WAS a memorable scene in Salisbury one market
day, a year or two ago, when a new bus station was to be
opened. The ceremony began with a luncheon in the
Council House, and then the Mayor of Salisbury, and I, as
Mayor of Wilton, proceeded formally to declare the station
open. We crossed the market place at the head of a small
procession, which grew rapidly as the assembled people
caught sight of our dignity and our chains, and eventually
arrived on the scene at the head of a considerable crowd.
Our first business was to cut two coloured ribbons which
had been stretched across the entrance to the station, and
then there immediately appeared the first bus which was
to use it. In order to prevent delay, this had filled up at its
old starting-point, and it was already crowded with
passengers for Andover. They had no idea they were going
to take part in any function. There they sat in their places,
hugging their parcels, and staring out of the windows with
astonishment at what must have looked to them like an
unruly crowd of rioters waiting to spring upon them.
Perhaps they were reassured by finding that the mob was
headed by two Mayors in their robes, each holding aloft a
pair of grape scissors. But their fears returned when these
Mayors addressed them with loud and passionate prayers:

'God bless this bus. May you have a safe journey. May

this bus pass safely through all the dangers of the road',
and other slogans equally suggesting that this particular
journey to Andover was likely to be a ticklish one.

*Salisbury was no stranger to civic occasions. A visit of the circuit
judges to preside at the assize courts was a good excuse for
some junketing. Here is Miss Child's version of events.*

THE TWO JUDGES expected, the High Sheriff's coach,
With himself and retainers, attend their approach:
Eighteen men, on horses, each a jav'lin in hand,
Are seen ready to follow their captain's command;
In their coats of dark blue, — and with waistcoats of red,
Of these worthies indeed it may truly be said,
That all wearing cocked hats, wondrous knowing and spruce,
To the pride of the cortege they greatly conduce,
As surrounding the carriage, — towards the high road,
Both with might and with main, hired horses they goad;
To the Weeping-cross tree, thus proceeding in state,
All there, with due patience, the arrival await;
And the Sheriff, as soon as their Lordships he spies,
(To show deepest respect for the learned and wise,)
Descends from his coach, where he offer them places,
Which the Judges accept, with bows and good graces;
While two trumpeters strain both their lungs and their cheeks
Certain sounds to emit, between screaming and shrieks;
Though I've often been told, that they certainly mean
To perform the fine anthem of 'God save the Queen'.

To the Council House come without any damage,
The steeds being carefully trained to the manage,
The commission to open, their Lordships proceed,
Then descant on good morals, in word and in deed:
And how it behoves them in their situation,
To hinder the crimes that dishonour the nation. —
Then comes Assize Sunday, a very fine thing,
For hundreds, nay thousands, of folks will it bring
From country around, and the villages near,
Where the churches are closed and no service they'll hear,
So that all may come hither, — to wonder and fear,
And to see my Lord Judge looking awfully big,
In his scarlet and ermine and well-powdered wig,
Proceeding to church midst the whole corporation,
His Worship the Mayor, and a large congregation.
From the pulpit they hear a most learned discourse,
Which the chaplain delivers with eloquent force;
And the Judges return, in the very same state
As two hours before, they passed through the Close Gate.

By the Bishop or Canons invited to dine
They then cheer up their spirits with capital wine,
For the very next morning their labours begin,
When they punish each knave, to reclaim him from sin;
And the harder the doom, — more kind the intention,
A remedy needful, to act as prevention,
And check in men's minds any wicked invention. —
They must arbitrate quarrels betwixt man and man,
With strict law and deep learning, the best way they can;
And on matters extremely important decide,

Which old friendships and int'rests may sadly divide.
All these toils being ended in three or four days,
Their carriage they order, and proceed on their ways
To the next county towns, — till circuits are ended,
Rejoicing in hope, that some wrongs are amended.

The assizes were one highlight of the social calendar. Two others, for the Salisbury aristocracy of the 1770s, were the summer race meeting and the autumn music festival. Mrs Harris, of Malmesbury House in the Close, described them both in letters to her son.

THURSDAY, the second day of the Salisbury races, the sport on the hill was good: it consisted in two races, one for the City plate, the other for fifty guineas given by the members for the city. The horses started alternately, which made it lively. In the evening there was a card assembly and a cotillon party; it was poorly attended, but those who were there were gentry, so the dancing was agreeable. Yesterday all went to the hill: two races again, one as usual for the Give-and-take plate, the other a sweepstake by subscription of 130 guineas, to be ridden by gentlemen, who were Lord Castlehaven, Mr George Hanger, Mr Basset, and young Compton. They all rode exceedingly well. Mr Hanger won, though the knowing ones say Lord Castlehaven's horse must have beat if his lordship had not been much frightened. Jostling was allowed, and Mr Hanger declared he would jostle and whip whoever came near: this menace intimidated Lord Castlehaven so much that he prudently kept at a due distance from George Hanger. These heroes rode but one heat, but it was very exciting, for everybody's attention was much more taken up with seeing gentlemen ride than jockeys. Have you received the box Mr Bate sent you some time since? I hope you will soon have it, or the buckles will be too small for the fashion, for George Hanger wore larger at the Salisbury race-balls.

OUR FESTIVAL is just ended, and we have brought things to a happy conclusion. I never remember so much good company, or a more numerous appearance. We had a rehearsal here Tuesday evening, and a most crowded room. That day the Bowles and the Buckleys dined here; Wednesday morning we rehearsed the Passione, Stabat Mater, &c. here, to another crowded audience. That day all the Professors dined with us, we ladies were obliged to assist at the dinner, as Madame Tenducci and Mrs and Miss Lindley were of the party, so, from the heat of the breakfast-room we got into a far greater heat in the dining-room; it was literally out of the frying-pan into the fire. The music began here that morning at ten, and never ceased till three. We eat, drank, dressed, and went to the Oratorio of Hercules, which went off charmingly. Tenducci is amazingly improved; in his part the old Handelian songs were left out, and some fine Italian ones smuggled in, in their places. Thursday Lady Pembroke called on us to go to the Messiah, which went off divinely.

As might be expected of Him, of course. And on the subject of religion, discerning visitors soon discover that the cathedral is not Salisbury's only spectacular church. St Thomas's, the city church, is a distinguished building, memorable for its remarkable medieval doom painting. The poet Clive Sansom has described it.

ABOVE the chancel arch
Rise roofs and palaces
Of the heavenly Jerusalem, with a rainbow
Spanning from tower to tower.
On it, aloof (a keystone
To the rainbow's Norman arch)
Sits Christ in glory: holy,
Magnificent, angel-attended,
Judging the quick and the dead.
To the right, below him, watching,
The twelve apostles; and under them
A graveyard garden, where the righteous
Rise up like tulips from their tombs.
To the left, sinwards, the damned.
They, too, would rise,
But hordes of pitchforked demons
Thrust them, naked, back,
Or drag them, screaming and lamenting,
To a flaming cauldron: miser
Clutching his money-bags,
Ale-wife with short measure,
Cornering merchant - all

Prodded and tossed like cornsheaves
Into the devouring flames...
A clear lesson to us all
Craning and gaping upwards
That even the patience of God
Is exhaustible, and repentance not merely
Virtuous but a sound investment,
Especially in middle age.

The Guildhall

Something like that sentiment must have run through the mind of the rector of another city church, St Edmund's (now the arts centre), one Thomas Naish. As he recorded in his diary:

31 DEC. the last day of the year 1695, I mett with a most violent clapp of thunder and lightning being in Catherine Street in Sarum about 7 a clock at night, and before I gott home I mett with a second much like the other. The next day I heard that it had done some mischiefe to my church of St Edmonds; there I found very remarkable things done chiefly about the towr. The dyall plate which hung up against the towr in the inside was thrown quite to the other end of the church being torne to pieces, and some of its splinters sticking in the wall near the communion table. There were severall cracks in the towr, chiefly where the bells hang, and upon the topp near the north west pinnacle, which was twisted something from its place. This may be reckoned a second deliverance of the people of this parish from danger and mischief; there was no person hurt though there were many at this same time in the towr ringing. Lord grant that we may make a thankfull use hereof, and adore thy majesty and goodness, and take all thy gentle admonitions, and turne them to our good by amending our lives and reforming our manners. From lightning and tempest good Lord deliver us. Amen.

Uppermost in his thoughts was an earlier, even more dramatic incident, which occurred in 1653. It was sonorously recorded in deliberate prose, in the pages of a volume of churchwardens' accounts.

JUNE 8: Upon vew of the weekenes of the tower by reason of the foundering of the foundation of the south west pillar they thinke fitte to ease the tower and to take of from it as much wayt or burthen they can, therefore do order th't the churchwarden do cause the bell upon the top of the tower and the frame in w'ch it hanges and the great massy wayt w'ch is the turrat wheron the coke [? cloke] standes to bee taken away and levell it flat and dispose of the bell and the frame of the turret and the lead for the benefitt of the church — the sexton shall ring the treable at 5 a clocke in the morning in the place of the other bell th't is ordered to bee taken downe and it is desired th't Mr John Ivie jun. do assist the churchwardens when they need him.

June 19. The whole parish as well as the vestry summoned. They find the tower to bee so clift w'th shaking, by meanes of the ringing of the belles, and that wee cannot without great danger of the towers falling downe suffer any peale to bee rung againe, and therfore to give ease to the sayd tower, it is now ordered that the churchwardens do take downe all the belles in the tower except the greatest bell to call the people together and the treeble to ring at 5 a clocke in the morning, and that this bee done w'th what speed possible that so the south west pillar may bee amended.

July 11. Amongst the many eminent mercyes that the inhabitantes of Edmundes parish have received wee may reckon the speciall providence of God whereby wee the parishioners and our familyes were saved from remarkeable and iminent danger on the sabbath day, being June the 26th one thousand six hundred fifty and three, when the maior, and many other principall inhabitantes of the citty w'th a great multitude of Godly Christianes weer mett at Edmundes church for the publique worshipe of God. The walles of the tower thereof were become ruinous, broken, and (by the unwary attemptes of some, who in order to reparation had uncovered the roofe and undermined some pillars) onely not fallen. The maine pillars did bulge out, and sensiblely shake: the cleftes in the walles were seen to open and shutt with ringing the sermon bell th't day neither weer there any considerable proppes under set to support it, so th't nothing but the very hand of God did keep the stones and timber from falling untill the next morning th't his one people were all secure at home, and then hee so sweetly ordered the fall of the tower th't (albeit many woorkemen were about it th't day) neither man, woman, nor child, received any hurt therby. When wee consider what God hath formerly permitted when the tower in Siloa fell: and when the church of Blake fryars in London fell upon a people mett as wee were for worship but in another religion: when we apprehend what danger wee were in though not sensible of it at th't time, how sad an outcry would have bine made (not in our parish only, but) in our citty (like the great cry

74

in Egypt) wher almost every house would have suffered in the death of so many if God had mingled our blood with our sacrifices th't day. And when wee seriously recollect and set before us all the circumstances of this our new salvation, we cannot but breake foorth into praise and say as salvation, and glory, and honour, and power unto the Lord our God. And in a lively sense of the mercy desiring to perpetuate the memory of it unto posterity th't so the generations to come may prayse God as wee the living do this day. Wee doe order and appoynt th't the twenty six day of June yearly shall bee unto the people of Edmundes parish a day of soleme and publique thankesgiving unto God for the same. And wee beseech our brethren of this and the following generationes by the mercyes of God to present themselves living sacrifices holy, acceptable unto God in ther reasonable service of him, th't day as long as ther shall bee one stone upon another in Edmundes church and an inhabitant left alive in Edmundes parish. And wee do farther order th't either in the windowes or the walles or the gates of our new builded church (if not in all of them) there bee made as shall bee thought fit some monuments of this late deliverance. That our walles may mention the salvation and our gates the praise of the Lord.

Sept.5. The foregoing to be entered in this booke.

We have sauntered through Salisbury in the company of writers famous and unknown. We have seen what the city has to offer through the eyes of visitors and residents. To whom should we give the last word? One of those egregious ladies of the Close, perhaps — Miss Child, who set out some 150 years ago to chronicle in bad verse the entire history of the city and cathedral she loved. This was her conclusion.

NOW in words of an adage, which truth has long claimed,
I'll inform you for what this old city is famed:

> The height of its steeple,
> The pride of its people,
> Good scissors and knives,
> And its beautiful wives.
> Buy a book, buy a book, now I merrily cry!
> Buy a book, buy a book, and for ever good bye!

Sources and Acknowledgements ~

The compiler wishes to express his gratitude to the staff of Salisbury and Trowbridge Local Studies Libraries, Bath Reference Library, and the University of Bristol Library, for affording research facilities; and to the copyright owners individually acknowledged below for permitting quotation from copyright items.

9-10: Richard Le Gallienne, *Travels in England*, 1900

10: Samuel Pepys, *The Diary of Samuel Pepys* (10th June 1668)

11: Daniel Defoe, *A tour thro' the whole island of Great Britain*, 3rd ed., 1742, vol.1

11-12: William Cobbett, *Rural Rides*, 1830

13: William Lisle Bowles, *The Poetical Works...* (ed. G. Gilfillan), vol.1, 1855

14: John Leland, *The itinerary...* (ed. L.T. Smith), vol.1, 1906

15-17: Walter Pope, *The Salisbury ballad...*, 1713 (reprinted 1770)

18-19: Latin text in *Wiltshire Archaeological and Natural History Magazine*, vol.57, 1959, pp.245-6 (newly translated)

20: W.H. Hudson, *A Shepherd's Life*, 1910

21: Ella Noyes, *Salisbury Plain*, 1913

22-3: William Golding, *The Spire*, 1964 (with permission, author's estate and Faber & Faber Ltd)

23-4: Maurice Hewlett, *Flowers in the grass*, 1920

25: Oliver Wendell Holmes, *Our hundred days in Europe*, 1887

26: J.J. Hissey, *Through ten English counties*, 1894

26-7: J.B. Priestley, *English Journey*, 1934

27-8: W.H. Hudson, *A Shepherd's Life*, 1910

28: Henry James, *English Hours*, 1905

29: W.H. Hudson, *Afoot in England*, 1909

29-31: Charles Kingsley, *Charles Kingsley: his letters and memories of his life, edited by his wife*, vol.1, 1877

32: Thomas Hardy, *Human shows, far phantasies, songs, and trifles*, 1925

33-4: William Cobbett, *Rural Rides*, 1830

34: Daniel Defoe, *A tour thro' the whole island of Great Britain*, 3rd ed., 1742, vol.1

35: Thomas Fuller, *The Worthies of England*, 1662

35-6: Miss Child, *The spinster at home in the Close of Salisbury: no fable...*, 6th ed., 1849

36: Edith Olivier, *Four Victorian Ladies of Wiltshire*, 1945 (with permission of Miss R. Olivier)

37: Charles Kingsley, *Charles Kingsley: his letters and memories of his life, edited by his wife*, vol.2, 1877

37-8: Oliver Wendell Holmes, *Our hundred days in Europe*, 1887

39: Nathaniel Hawthorne, *Our old home, and English notebooks*, vol.2, 1884

39,41: Edith Olivier, *Without knowing Mr Walkley: personal memories*, 1938 (with permission of Miss R. Olivier)

42: Charles Kingsley, *Charles Kingsley: his letters and memories of his life, edited by his wife*, vol.2, 1877

42: G.M. Young, *Portrait of an age: Victorian England*, 2nd ed., 1953

43-4: Coventry Patmore, *The Angel in the House*, 1854

45: Dorothy Devenish, *A Wiltshire home: a study of Little Durnford*, 1948 (with permission of Batsford & Co.)

46-7: Anthony Trollope, *The Warden*, 1855

47-8: Thomas Hardy, *Jude the Obscure*, 1895

49: Richard Le Gallienne, *Travels in England*, 1900

50-1: Francis Kilvert, *Kilvert's Diary* (ed. W.Plomer), vol.3, 1940

52: Ernest Walls, *The Salisbury Avon*, 1929

53: John Aubrey, *The Natural History of Wiltshire*, 1847

53: Daniel Defoe, *A tour thro' the whole island of Great Britain*, 3rd ed., 1742, vol.1

53: Celia Fiennes, *The journeys...* (ed. C.Morris), 1949

53-4: Nathaniel Hawthorne, *Our old home, and English notebooks*, vol.2, 1884

54: Thomas Fuller, *The worthies of England*, 1662

55: William Schellink, *The journal...* (ed. M. Exwood and H.L. Lehmann), Camden Soc, 5th series, vol.1, 1993

55-6: Samuel Pepys, *The Diary of Samuel Pepys* (11th June 1668)

56: John Byng, *The Torrington Diaries...* (ed. C.B. Andrews), vol.1, 1934

56-9: Charles Dickens, *Martin Chuzzlewit*, 1843-4

59-61: Thomas Hardy, 'On the Western Circuit', in *Life's Little Ironies*, 1903

61,63: Dorothy Devenish, *A Wiltshire home: a study of Little Durnford*, 1948 (with permission of Batsford & Co.)

63-4: W.H. Hudson, *A Shepherd's Life*, 1910

65-6: Edith Olivier, *Country moods and tenses*, 1941 (with permission of Miss R. Olivier)

66-8: Miss Child, *The spinster at home in the Close of Salisbury: no fable...*, 6th ed., 1849

68-9: Earl of Malmesbury, *A series of letters of the 1st Earl of Malmesbury*, vol.1, 1870

70-1: Clive Sansom, *The Cathedral*, 1958 (with permission of Methuen & Co.)

72: Thomas Naish, *The diary...* (ed. D.Slatter), Wiltshire Record Soc, vol.20, 1965 (with permission of the Society)

73-5: H.J.F. Swayne (ed.), *Churchwardens' accounts of S.Edmund and S.Thomas, Sarum, 1443-1702...*, 1896

76: Miss Child, *The spinster at home in the Close of Salisbury: no fable...*, 6th ed., 1849

A Miscellany of Explanations ~

aiguille: a sharply-pointed mountain peak

bete: foolish (French)

Chimborazo: a mountain in Ecuador, one of the highest peaks in the Andes

Cold Harbour: land west of the Avon, between Old Sarum and Wilton

Constable painting: Salisbury Cathedral, by John Constable (1776-1837), English landscape painter

Devil-a-bit: a jocular colloquial phrase meaning a firm negative

gree: 'the wind flings his gree', i.e. the wind shows his might or superiority

Harnham: suburb of Salisbury south of the river

Kelmscott: Oxfordshire home, from 1871, of the poet, craftsman and socialist, William Morris

kennel: surface drain or gutter of a street

Kington and Langley: Kington St Michael and Langley Burrell, villages near Chippenham, north Wiltshire

Laverstoke: now spelled Laverstock, village east of Salisbury

'lot had fallen unto them...': allusion to Psalm 16 verse 7 (Book of Common Prayer)

Melchester: Hardy's name for Salisbury

Oratorio of Hercules: by Handel, first performed in London 1745. Handel was a close friend of members of the Harris family

ordinary: a fixed price pub meal

Osmund, Saint: builder of Old Sarum cathedral, his relics venerated after his death (1099); canonized 1457

Pandulfo: Cardinal Pandulf (died 1226), papal legate to England when Salisbury Cathedral was begun

punk: obsolete word meaning prostitute

Rogation: Christian festival and procession which took place immediately before Ascension Day

shriving: hearing confession, and conferring absolution

Tenducci: G.F. Tenducci (died 1790), famous Italian male soprano

Weeping Cross Tree: tree at the north-eastern approach to Salisbury (near present St Mark's roundabout), supposedly where travellers bid their farewells

Wilton: small town west of Salisbury, which had an important nunnery

Index ~